COLLABORATION
Soup

A SIX-STEP RECIPE FOR CO-CREATIVE MEETINGS AND OTHER CONVERSATIONS

DELIA HORWITZ & PAULA VIGNEAULT

ISBN: 1449907679
ISBN-13: 9781449907679

Preface

Have you ever sat through a long, boring meeting, just waiting for the business to be over so you could leave? Maybe you've been in meetings where great ideas were expressed, but nothing ever came of them. Perhaps a few people dominated, or the outcome was already decided, leaving little room for your input.

You may be reading this because you've had similar experiences and are looking for a better way. If so, you've made a good choice. We wrote *Collaboration Soup* to provide a simple, brief and practical guide for planning, leading, and participating in successful collaborative meetings and events. It contains our favorite methods and techniques learned during our 25-plus years of collaborative experiences with a wide range of business, government and community clients.

We were inspired by the classic fable *Stone Soup*. It's the story of villagers in a time of famine who are suspicious of a stranger they fear will take what little food they have. To their surprise, the stranger sets a pot of water to boil in the village square, adds a stone from his pocket, and exclaims loudly that he plans to make a delicious stone soup to share with them all. Then he explains that the soup would be even better with some vegetables, spices, or a bit of meat. First a few and then many villagers come forward to offer what they have into the pot. After the soup is cooked, they enjoy a nourishing meal together. By contributing what they can, they create something they all care about that they could not create individually.

Collaboration Soup uses the metaphor of *Stone Soup* and presents an easy six-step recipe for creating the conditions to draw out the collective wisdom and brilliance of a group. If you are not a cook, or don't particularly enjoy cooking, look beyond the cooking examples to use the ideas and directions contained within these pages.

Imagine yourself using this recipe in your business, government, non-profits, communities, religious organizations, educational institutions, homeowner associations and families to:

- Plan for the future
- Identify new solutions
- Prioritize needs or resources
- Address complex issues
- Resolve a neighborhood or community issue
- Create shared goals
- Develop a group's budget priorities
- Discover new ways to implement change
- Conduct a retreat
- Organize a party or social event

By applying the six-step recipe in *Collaboration Soup*, you can turn your boring and frustrating meetings into practical and enjoyable collaborative experiences. This guide will support you every step along the way.

Introduction

"One hundred ordinary people can come up with a better solution than one wise person."   The Dalai Lama

Many people today are hungry for new and sustaining solutions to business, environmental, and social challenges. Many of us feel drawn to participate in our communities, asking what we can do together to meet those challenges. Business and organizational managers want to find ways to stimulate their teams to work more effectively together. Government officials tell us they want to hear about our needs, our ideas, and our priorities. We are coming forward as never before to participate and seek solutions that can benefit us all.

But how do we do that? How do we overcome traditions of authoritarian leadership, top-down hierarchy, or individual self-interest, which are typical of how meetings and many conversations are conducted? Whether in an organization, a family, or in our communities, the problems of today are so complex that no one person has all the answers. In this age of complexity, how do we bring people together to have meaningful conversations in which they are satisfied with the experience as well as the outcome?

We do this by creating the conditions for people to talk with each other in ways that honor each other's differences and combine their individual ideas. We do this by asking different kinds of questions and deeply listening so that previously unimagined possibilities can emerge. This type of conversation is collaboration at its best, and we refer to it as co-creative.

Let us explain what we mean by the terms collaboration and co-creative, which we use throughout this guide. Simply put, collaboration means to work together. Co-creative takes that definition one-step further to indicate working together in a way that blends the wisdom and brilliance of each individual to create something new that is owned by all, similar to the villagers in the *Stone Soup* fable mentioned earlier. Being part of a co-creative conversation can elevate our experience to one of hope and optimism; showing us that together we can discover possibilities and solutions that might not be possible by any one individual.

Co-creative conversations are nothing new. The qualities and abilities necessary for people working together collaboratively are intrinsic and innate to all. Collaboration is universally applicable to almost any shared human endeavor. Putting those abilities into practice is a learnable skill, and with practice, we can all learn to be effective at serving up a new and better kind of conversation whenever people come together for a shared purpose.

Collaboration Soup will show you how to engage in co-creative conversations that address your most critical issues. As professional facilitators and group process leaders, we have condensed our knowledge and years of experience into this simple six-step recipe so you can cook up your own great group events and meetings.

Collaboration Soup is written in five parts:
- Part I: Getting Started introduces the six-step recipe, key roles, and information on the collaborative brain.
- Part II: The Recipe presents each step and gives you basic directions for how to carry out each role.
- Part III: Tips and Tools contains suggestions for fundamental aspects of an effective collaborative event.
- Part IV: Our Favorite Methods, Processes and Activities includes detailed directions for how to maximize productive and enjoyable interactions.
- Part V: Troubleshooting contains suggestions for difficult circumstances that may occur.

Don't be afraid to jump in and use these steps—they work! We have seen people who thought they had nothing in common end their collaborative conversation feeling good about each other and committing to shared action in ways no one could have anticipated. Give it a try. We encourage you to invite people into your kitchen to add their ingredients and spices to whatever it is you are cooking up–and discover the joy of successful collaboration.

Table of Contents

PART I: GETTING STARTED

Recipe for Collaboration
Soup: An Overview

The recipe for *Collaboration Soup* has six steps. In each step, we give you directions that contain practical ideas and information for use in creating your own collaborative events. You can follow these directions precisely, adapt them, use parts, or be inspired to cook up your own unique dish.

Attitude is everything. We all know that food tastes better when made with care, so bring your good will, acceptance, and creativity with you to the collaboration kitchen. Your thoughts and behaviors are like the spices and herbs that turn an ordinary conversation into a delicious gourmet experience with productive results. We encourage you to be playful and curious, open and flexible, expecting the unexpected at every turn. As the ingredients are allowed to cook thoroughly, avoid shortcuts that come from impatience or judgment, and watch as new flavorful ideas emerge and blend.

Here is an overview of the six steps:

Step 1. **Ready to Go**. It all begins with a need or a desire, and then proceeds to enrolling others in the planning.

Step 2. **Engage Your Group**. This involves inviting participants, creating the agenda, and assembling helpful tools and resources.

Step 3. **Cook the Conversation**. Individuals come together using effective processes to share and blend their ideas.

Step 4. **Integrate the Ideas**. The group identifies the common themes and pauses to acknowledge and celebrate what has been co-created.

Step 5. **Plan the Action**. The group discusses possible next steps and creates a plan to implement the co-created ideas.

Step 6. **End with Clarity**. The details are wrapped up, closing comments are shared, plans are made to create and distribute a Summary Document, and the meeting place is put back in order.

You will get the best results by using all six steps. However, it is important to respond to the changing needs of any group, so be flexible, spontaneous, and creative—and enjoy the adventure.

Hot Tips and How to Identify Them

Throughout this guide, **Hot Tips** are indicated by a wooden spoon. Each time the Hot Tips wooden spoon appears, it is asking you to pay attention to a valuable and important tip. Similar to when cooking a soup, if you forget to stir the pot at key points, the ingredients may not mix well together and might burn.

Three Cooks in the Kitchen

In the *Stone Soup* story we spoke of earlier, the stranger announces he is making soup, supplies a stone to get it started, and invites the villagers to participate. In collaborative meetings, we call this role the **Convener**. The pot or vessel that holds the soup makes it easy for people's ideas to mix and blend. This is the role of the **Facilitator**. The villagers who gather to add their ingredients are the **Contributors**. In each of the six steps described in Part II, there are directions for these roles—the three cooks in the kitchen.

The **Convener** is like the hungry stranger in the story who brings people together and invites them to create something more than what he or she can make alone. The stone is his or her seed idea that holds the promise of the soup. A person in the role of convener offers a topic and/or a purpose for the conversation and then lets go of controlling the results. After the convener's initial actions, which include forming a team and planning the first meeting, he or she may want to participate as a contributor.

The **Facilitator** is similar to the iron pot—even-tempered and able to hold all the ingredients in a way that allows them to blend and cook well together. A good facilitator supports everyone to contribute their best thinking by asking relevant questions, encouraging interaction, and listening in a way that draws out the group's wisdom.

It is essential that the facilitator remain neutral about the issues, keeping his or her own personal opinions out of the conversation. If the facilitator needs to give an opinion, he or she needs to make it clear when they are stepping out of, and back into, the facilitator role.

Many people have a natural ability to be an effective facilitator. There may be times, however, due to the topic or the intensity of opinions, when having a more trained and skilled professional facilitator is in the best interest of the group.

The **Contributors** are similar to the villagers in the story. By offering what they have and accepting what others bring, they co-create a meal that would not have been possible without combining their individual ingredients. Maintaining a spirit of open-mindedness, acceptance, curiosity and sincerity allows contributors to achieve shared goals and accomplish amazing results.

While the above three roles describe the main cooks in the kitchen, there are two additional and very helpful roles:

The **Scribe**, sometimes called the recorder, takes notes.

The **Timekeeper** keeps track of the time.

It is important to realize that everyone present in a collaborative conversation is a contributor who affects the outcome. As each person takes responsibility for being a positive contributor, quality conversations are co-created where ideas merge to become effective positive actions. People leave this type of meeting feeling valued, included and respected.

Your Collaborative Brain

Recent scientific discoveries give us clues about how to access collaborative thinking. Understanding how your brain works to help or hinder the collaborative process is fundamental to any successful co-creative meeting or discussion.

Collaborative activities require the use of your prefrontal cortex (PFC), the part of your brain that distinguishes humans from all other animals. The PFC is located on the very top of your brain, positioned just behind your forehead, and is the part of your brain responsible for choice, foresight, and emotional balance.

However, there is another side to the story. A part of the brain known as the amygdala, associated with your primitive brain, can have a negative effect on your ability to think and act collaboratively. The amygdala acts like a switching station, constantly evaluating incoming signals and triggering protective reactions to real or imagined threats. The "fight or flight" response is an example of what happens when you perceive yourself to be in danger.

In the *Stone Soup* story, when the villagers first meet the stranger, they are afraid he will take what little food they have and they tell him to leave. The stranger reassures the villagers by exclaiming loudly that he plans to make a delicious stone soup to share with them all. Their fears are calmed by his offer and they are willing to contribute what they have, trusting they will all be fed—an example of PFC thinking.

Throughout this guide, you will be given suggestions; guidelines for creating and supporting the conditions that help make you and others feel safe. By using them, you will minimize the chances of an amygdala "fight or flight" takeover, and maximize access to higher brain abilities.

The chart below gives further information about the differences between the two.

PREFRONTAL CORTEX (PFC) VIEW	AMYGDALA VIEW
Sees the whole picture.	Tells us if we are safe or not.
Makes possible a wide variety of thinking, feeling, and behavior options.	Automatically triggers survival thinking and behaviors.
Makes choices to balance what you want with what others want.	Alters your behavior to protect you and look out for your own interests.
Notices and cares about the impact of your behavior on others.	Focuses on self-preservation, saying and doing things without thinking about the effect on others.
Opens you to empathy and compassion.	Triggers blame, judgment, defensiveness, hostility.
Helps you tune in to your intuition and insight.	Uses information to calculate and analyze.
Helps your ability to imagine a different future.	Protects your current "safe" position.
Monitors your fearful thoughts and helps maintain emotional balance.	Triggers automatic "fight or flight" responses.

How to Use the Collaboration Soup Recipe

When to Use It

You can use the *Collaboration Soup* recipe in a variety of situations— sitting around the dinner table to plan a family vacation, accomplishing team goals at work, or working with hundreds of people at a community forum. This recipe works well to:

- Do strategic or project planning
- Identify a shared vision
- Set group goals
- Brainstorm and get everyone's ideas on the table
- Merge different points of view
- Combine resources
- Reduce overlap or merge duplicate services
- Get unstuck when you are unsure of the answer or solutions
- Resolve differing or apparently competing opinions or positions
- Discover something new and as yet unknown

As you can see, this recipe can be used with great versatility. Jump in and give it a try.

When *Not* to Use It

Collaboration as a strategy for effective meetings may not always be your best choice. To determine if collaboration is the best choice for your event, be honest about how much power or authority the group has to implement any decisions made. We suggest you do not call your method collaboration unless you intend to value, respect and include every person's ideas.

You may want to use other methods or approaches if your purpose for gathering people together is to:

- Give project updates
- Give assignments
- Present or clarify information
- Explain your idea
- Get feedback on plans already underway
- Get sponsorship for, or participation in, an idea whose outcome is already decided

Another situation where this recipe may not be effective involves people or groups so attached to their position that even with the most expert facilitator—and most members of the group sincerely wanting to include all perspectives—collaboration is not possible. People need to be as committed to finding common ground as they are to maintaining their positions. The six-step recipe in *Collaboration Soup* will not be effective if some of the people involved are determined to make dessert and not soup.

ᕇᕤ

Knowing When to Walk Away

If you have ever been part of a Homeowner's Association, you may have observed something like the following. When I lived in a condominium, I became aware that two homeowners were arguing about whether or not to replace the 25-year-old air conditioning unit that served both their apartments. One owner wanted to replace it. The other owner did not think it was necessary, and would not agree to pay for his half. Being the collaboration specialist I was, I thought I could help them come to an amiable agreement.

I offered to facilitate their conversations in the interest of preserving neighborly harmony, and I was quite optimistic. However, after three meetings in which we repeatedly discussed many options, I realized neither homeowner was willing to change his original position in order to find a mutually agreeable solution. The dispute resulted in a court settlement that included legal fees. Each party ended up paying their half, which totaled more than the original cost. Other neighbors took sides. So much for neighborly harmony.

Had I realized earlier that collaboration was not going to be possible, it would have saved me time and energy. I learned a good lesson about when to walk away.

Now you are ready to begin. Part II will take you through the steps of your collaborative event.

PART II: THE RECIPE

Step 1. Ready to Go

Careful planning in the beginning will make it easier to put the co-created ideas into action later on. Take time to set a good foundation. Similar to when you plan a meal, consider: What kind of ingredients will go into your soup? Where will the ingredients come from? How will you gather them? How will you combine them for a delicious outcome? All of these decisions and more need to be considered before it's time to convene the meeting and stir the pot.

The more people and points of view you include during the planning phase, the more support you will have when it is time to implement the results. The amount of alignment of the planners before the meeting or event will set the tone for what follows. Alignment does not mean people have to be in 100% agreement. However, it is important that everyone is going in the same general direction, even if each person has a little different "spin" or is going at a different pace. For example, when cooks are aligned on making soup—not salad or dessert—everyone contributes something to produce a soup and no one brings lettuce.

CONVENER ROLE

As the person with the initial idea, your role during the planning step is to get things started. The following directions will help you do that.

1. Be clear on your purpose for calling the meeting. Be prepared to honestly share that purpose with others.

2. Consider inviting others to join an event planning team and be part of the planning process. Here are some pointers for forming a planning team:

- Six people or less works best.
- Select people who share your passion for the topic, and who are willing and able to work cooperatively.
- Include your facilitator if that person has been selected.
- Make sure people who are on the planning team understand their responsibilities, including expected time commitments.
3. The event planning team will then:
    - Clarify the purpose of the proposed meeting or event. The following questions will be helpful in bringing about alignment on the purpose:
        - Why are you calling this meeting?
        - What is the topic to be discussed?
        - What is the opportunity or possibility?
    - Identify people, groups or organizations who are key stakeholders, for example:
        - People invited to the event.
        - People who have an interest in the outcome of the event or project.
        - Those who may experience the impact of decisions made at the event.
    - Survey some or all of the key stakeholders in advance to identify their important issues and desired outcomes. You can do this in person, by phone, or using electronic or paper surveys. Don't assume that you see the issue the same way others see it. As the agenda is planned, include multiple stakeholders' perspectives.
    - Choose a location and time for the meeting that best suits the invited participants. A neutral location is best when you have divided factions.

Hot Tip

Survey stakeholders before the meeting, and include their needs and interests as you plan. Set an example of respect and good listening as you solicit diverse points of view.

FACILITATOR ROLE

Your role is to:

1. Be in close communication with the convener and the event planning team.
2. Use information gathered from the stakeholders and work with the event planning team to begin creating an agenda. You will need to decide:
   - Discussion questions
   - Activities and processes
   - The time planned for each section of the agenda. *Note*: Be sure to leave plenty of time at the end for creating an action plan with next steps and accountabilities.

CONTRIBUTOR ROLE

If you are surveyed as a stakeholder during the planning step, be sure to:

1. Contribute your ideas honestly.
2. Respond in a timely way so your input can be included.

◈

Your Stakeholders Know What They Need – Ask Them

We facilitated a strategic planning effort for a 35-person advisory board appointed by a County Board of Supervisors. They were responsible for making recommendations related to several million dollars of federal funds for economic development. Attendance at the group's board meetings had been sparse and active involvement from these busy business, government and non-profit executives was minimal. Because the group only met every other month, they barely knew each other, and the meetings were mostly a report from the director about finances.

When the director asked if anybody had anything to add, there was often silence. He was frustrated that their wisdom and community connections were not being tapped, and he thought they didn't care. After speaking with each board member, we discovered that they were as frustrated as the Director, and wanted more involvement. They wanted to know that their participation was creating positive results.

Using information gathered during this stakeholder survey, we facilitated one four-hour meeting in which they revised their mission, agreed on several clear and achievable goals, and identified accountabilities and measures. After that experience, their meetings became very lively with people contributing ideas and resources. Attendance skyrocketed.

Even short meetings can be very effective when you let the stakeholders influence the agenda.

Step 2. Engage Your Group

Like any host or hostess who plans a dinner, you want your guests to look forward to attending. Invite people to your event in a way that encourages their involvement. Make sure everyone has the same information and understands how important their participation is.

Variety adds spice to any dish; so cast your net wide. Remain open to the unique input of many different points of view. If you are hesitant or reluctant to invite people you think may disagree, don't let that fear keep them out of the conversation. The sooner you engage them, the more likely they are to contribute. Remember, everything goes into the pot.

CONVENER ROLE

At this stage, the event planning team is working with the convener to do the following:

1. Create the final list of who will be invited. This list will likely include the stakeholders you surveyed in Step 1, and perhaps others. Think about who could contribute to, or further the issue you are focusing on. Invite specific individuals, or send invitations to an organization and ask them to send a representative. Don't forget to ask others who they think should be added to your list.
2. Extend the invitation and include all relevant information, such as:
    *   The date, location, start and end times and who to contact for information.
    *   The purpose of the meeting and the activities planned.
    *   Who the planners, sponsors and invitees are.
    *   Background information on the issue, including websites to check, reports to read, or statistics you have gathered.

3. Plan how to organize the meeting room to optimize collaboration. Make a list of supplies and resources such as food, tables and chairs, easels and chart paper, nametags, paper and pens, microphones, computer and projector or other equipment, and identify who will bring what. You will find a suggestion section for Setting Up the Room for Success in Part III: Tips and Tools.

4. Identify people needed for various tasks, such as leading small groups, taking notes, keeping time, running technological equipment, setting up and cleaning up, etc.

5. Send a confirmation or reminder about the event a few days before.

Hot Tip

Carefully consider how the invitation is extended, and by whom, to increase the likelihood that all perspectives will be present. When people arrive having the same information, it saves time, minimizes confusion, and reduces conflicts.

FACILITATOR ROLE

Your role is to work closely with the convener and the event planning team to understand their purposes for holding the event or meeting. Begin carefully considering what activities and discussion questions would accomplish those purposes. Include the information you have about stakeholders' concerns. As you plan the agenda activities, go to the Tips and Tools and Our Favorite Methods, Processes and Activities sections in Part III and Part IV for helpful and detailed suggestions.

CONTRIBUTOR ROLE

Your role is to contribute if you choose to accept an invitation. Here are some suggestions:

1. Respond to the invitation by the requested date indicating if you will attend or not.

2. If asked, recommend other possible contributors to invite.

3. Before bringing guests, confirm it is okay to do so.
4. Arrange your calendar to be on time and plan to stay until the end.
5. Review the materials sent to you before you arrive.
6. Call if you will be late or must cancel.
7. Realize how important your unique contribution is and carefully consider what ideas and attitudes you will bring.

Tell The Whole Story In The Invitation

A colleague and I convened a year-long community leadership program designed to bring people with opposing views or differing political agendas together to build relationships, learn from each other and develop their collaborative leadership skills. Three hundred civic and community leaders were invited to focus groups to discuss what topics would be included in the curriculum. We thought attendance would be high if the invitation came from the President of the Chamber of Commerce and asked her to send it. I was shocked to learn that key stakeholders were not attending our events because they believed the program was a platform for furthering the Chamber's pro-growth agenda. I could not understand where they got that idea until I personally talked with an environmental leader who told me that people made this assumption because the invitation came from the Chamber of Commerce.

When I explained that professional facilitators would lead the focus groups and program, and that we were dedicated to lessening the hostility and fragmentation in the community, he agreed to attend. Word spread about our real purpose and credentials, and attendance soared.

I learned that it is important to consider what assumptions invitees might make, and to include the who and why, as well as the what and where, in the invitation.

Step 3. Cook the Conversation

Once people have responded to your invitation and come together for your meeting or event, it's time to put the pot on the fire and start "cookin' the soup. A good soup depends on all the ingredients blending well together to produce a uniquely flavored dish. No one ingredient can dominate the other, and each ingredient is important for what it adds to the final outcome. Likewise, in co-creative conversations, each person's input is a valuable contribution to the final product, promising to deliver a sum greater than its parts – a tasty blend of many flavors.

The attitude people bring to the conversation is very important. Have you ever eaten an elaborate meal and when finished, felt unsatisfied? Or maybe you have had a simple meal that was cooked with loving care, and you felt like you had eaten a feast. Conversations can be like this, too. When all participants—convener, facilitator and contributors—bring an attitude of caring, appreciation, optimism and openness, it infuses the conversation with a tasty good will.

CONVENER ROLE

As the person who has initiated the meeting, you should be the first to address the group. Model the attitudes and behaviors that will be requested of everyone.

1. In your opening remarks, explain honestly why you have initiated this conversation, who else was involved in the planning, any financial sponsors, how invitees were selected, and perhaps your hopes. Honest sharing helps sooth concerns people may have.

2. Let the group know if you will join them as a contributor once your opening remarks are complete.
3. Introduce the facilitator and provide a brief background about him or her.

FACILITATOR ROLE

The following is a list of steps we recommend to create the conditions for effective co-creative conversation. Remember, it is important to stay flexible so you can include unexpected ideas the group agrees to pursue.

1. Welcome people and thank them for attending.
2. Request everyone turn off his or her cell phone or pager.
3. Do an opening, or brain lifter exercise. For examples, see Arrival, Brain Lifter and Opening Exercises in Part IV: Our Favorite Methods, Processes and Activities
4. Give basic logistics information, such as where the bathrooms are located, when there will be a break, any information about food, etc. When people are oriented to their surroundings, the higher brain we refer to in Part I (the PFC) can function more effectively.
5. Confirm that everyone has received the background material. Have extra copies to distribute if needed.
6. Get everyone's agreement to follow attitude and behavior guidelines. Start with those listed below, or have the group create their own. Keep a large and legible chart posted of the guidelines they have agreed to, and remind people of them if needed.

SAMPLE GUIDELINES

- Be brief
- Stay on the topic
- One person speaks at a time
- Listen without interrupting
- Be respectful
- Suspend judgment

---

7. Review the planned agenda with the group. Ask if anyone has something to add or clarify, and adjust the plan as needed in order to gain alignment of the entire group. Gaining alignment now makes it less likely that the group will get sidetracked or go off on tangents. In reviewing the agenda, include the following points:
   - The purpose, vision, possibility, or issue
   - The planned activities
   - The planned ending time

8. Briefly explain the responsibilities of the people who have specific roles, for example:
   - The *Facilitator* moves the conversations along in respectful and time efficient ways, making sure everyone has a chance to speak. The facilitator is neutral and inclusive, and does not judge what others say or add his or her own opinions.
   - The *Contributors* follow the agreed upon guidelines and participate in the conversation.
   - The *Timekeeper* helps the group stay on time.
   - The *Scribe* captures people's ideas, the common themes, any decisions or action items, and general notes, in writing.

Hot Tip for the Scribe

It is important for everyone to feel that his or her ideas are being included. Use large wall charts to write people's words in large bold letters. It is acceptable to shorten their statements, but be sure to use their words. Have a separate secondary wall chart to record side topics or points off the main purpose (sometimes called the "parking lot") so even contributions that are not about the topic are acknowledged. You will find suggestions for Note Taking and Using Flip Charts in Part III: Tips and Tools.

9. Acknowledge to the group there are two dimensions to co-creative collaboration—interaction and action, which are equally valuable. Some people find discussion and the way in which the work is

accomplished more engaging, while others are drawn to making action plans. Here are various ways you could describe this continuum, and some suggestions for discussing the differences and contributions of each:

CONTINUUM OF CO-CREATIVE CONVERSATIONS	
INTERACTION	ACTION
Discussions	Decisions
Relationships	Tasks
The journey	The destination
How people are interacting	What gets done
Feelings, social and emotional needs	Goals and outcomes
Planning	Doing
Process	Action

- A fun way to get people involved and acknowledge the value of both is to have people raise their hands to indicate which side of the continuum is more comfortable for them.
- You can ask the group to add their own words to the two columns.
- Encourage the more action-oriented people to have patience for the extra time needed to have inclusive conversations. Encourage the more discussion-oriented people to be willing to move on to decisions and actions.

10. Clarify and agree on the decision-making method. You will find suggestions for Deciding How to Decide and Defining Alignment in Part III: Tips and Tools.

11. Get the group's agreement to proceed.

If there is disagreement about the planned agenda, it will be difficult to proceed in a collaborative way. Ask those who are not aligned what they need in order to proceed. If possible, modify the agenda to include their concerns.

12. Lead the group through the planned activities and discussion questions. Be flexible in adjusting the plan. You will find suggestions for various processes to use and a section on Creating Good Discussion Questions in Part IV: Our Favorite Methods, Processes, and Activities.

CONTRIBUTOR ROLE

In this step, you have a huge opportunity to help shape and influence the outcome of the event, not only by your spoken words but also by your behavior. Be aware that your attitude and mood are as important as what you say or do, your education, title, age, or experience.

Follow the agreed upon guidelines. Here is a more detailed explanation of the guidelines suggested above:

1. **Stay focused**. Stay present mentally as well as physically during discussions. Bring your attention back to the group whenever you notice your mind wandering. Be sure and turn off your cell phone or pager.
2. **Be curious**. Be willing to be surprised and to expand or even change your viewpoint.
3. **Speak clearly and briefly**, one person at a time. Make your key point without repeating yourself or rambling. Share your perspective as your perspective, not as "the truth."
4. **Listen** thoroughly without interrupting, and without planning your response, so you can hear someone's meaning as well as his or her words.
5. **Be respectful.** It's possible to appreciate that a person is contributing their point of view even if you don't agree with it.
6. **Notice your judgmental thoughts** as you have them, but don't voice them.
7. **Be open-minded.** Be willing to consider and include other viewpoints. Remember, in a co-creative conversation, all contributions have value.
8. **Ask questions** to help clarify and understand, rather than to criticize or persuade.
9. **Monitor your body reactions and emotions** to keep your higher brain in charge. If you notice yourself becoming agitated and moving into fight, flight or freeze behaviors, take some deep breaths, or get up and move around. Don't let your reactions carry you away. Re-focus and return to being curious as soon as you can.

Hot Tip for Everyone

Ask yourself: "Does what I want to say support having a collaborative discussion?" Or, "Might my words or actions throw water on the fire or cause a distraction?" In a co-creative conversation, it is the role of every person at the meeting to take full and equal responsibility for how their words, actions, and even facial expressions and body language impact the group.

HOW TO KNOW WHEN THE SOUP IS COOKED

How do you know when your conversation is finished and it's time to move on? Determining when to move to the next step can be challenging. So where do you stop? Again, we say, stay flexible. Be prepared to alter your timing as well as the activities planned, because the conversation may be complete sooner or later than you planned. The important point here is to stay tuned in—both as facilitator and as contributors—to your sense that the soup is done and it is time to take the conversation "off the stove." It is important to recognize when the conversation is complete for the moment and proceed to the next step of acknowledging the collective efforts and accomplishments.

Things to be aware of in determining if it is time to end this part of the conversation:

- **Overheating:** People are arguing. **Solution:** Slow down, acknowledge each person's contribution and encourage more listening.
- **Overcooking:** The same ideas are being repeated, and people are getting frustrated or impatient. **Solution:** Restate what ideas have already been presented or agreed upon and, if time allows, invite only new or different ideas.
- **Undercooking:** Everyone has not been heard, or commonalities are not yet apparent. **Solution:** Finish getting everyone's input, and continue asking the group to identify common themes.

Finding a Shared Purpose

In the 1980's, the director of a small airport hired me to facilitate a collaborative approach for airport expansion and long term planning in an environmentally sensitive habitat. She invited 25 property owners and representatives of federal, state, county and city government regulatory agencies to a meeting. The property owners included a state university, a national electronics corporation, independent farmers, and homeowners. Traditionally, each property owner developed its own expansion plans and dealt with each regulatory agency independently, arguing any disputes in public hearings or in court.

I wish I had a video of the facial expressions as the people arrived for their first meeting and realized who was there! They were highly suspicious of why they were invited. It took most of that first meeting for the group to identify a shared purpose they all cared about discussing. Rather than focus on the airport expansion, I had them identify their common interest, which was a healthy habitat.

They decided to develop one coordinated master plan that would consider all their concerns. Once they completed that plan, they formed an advisory group that is still working cooperatively for the habitat's benefit 25 years later.

It was important to find a shared purpose that included each group's interests and concerns.

Step 4. Integrate the Ideas

The soup is finally done and the pot is off the fire. It's time to put the meal on the table and enjoy what has been cooked. In a collaborative event, this step is about savoring what the group has co-created by identifying or confirming common themes, acknowledging the group's accomplishments and taking a few moments to celebrate.

Each contributor has an opportunity to experience being like a grain of sand on the beach as well as being the whole beach—feeling both a part of the whole and the whole itself—simultaneously. This dual awareness often brings about an "Aha!" moment of connection and unity. A new burst of energy is common and the power of the group's collective wisdom is visible. The higher brain (PFC) can now see connections and possibilities for positive action.

While it takes many hours to plan, gather the ingredients and cook the soup, as we all know, eating a meal can go very quickly. It is important to acknowledge and celebrate what has been cooked.

Bon Appétit!

FACILITATOR ROLE

Your job here is to help everyone own and celebrate the experience, as well as the information shared, before moving on to the action planning step.

Hot Tip

Keep your antennae out for those moments when the group becomes united. It might be a collective "Aha!" with everyone seeing the same thing at the same time, or several people saying the same thing at the same time. Whenever you sense this occurring, pause and have the group acknowledge their experience of unity.

1. Lead a discussion to identify and summarize common themes from the previous conversations. Doing this will put "the meal on the table," so to speak. Simply having a conversation in which everyone says what he or she thinks and then leaves is not co-creative collaboration. If the ideas discussed so far are written on wall charts, you can point the group's attention to the charts and ask them to identify the similarities. Examples of effective questions to ask are:
   - What are the commonalities?
   - What words are coming up most often as the group talks about this?
   - What are the similar ideas?
2. Create new charts that display the common themes.
3. Celebrate! Have the group reflect on their experience of the collaboration process so far. Encourage a spontaneous expression to acknowledge a sense of shared ownership and completion. It could simply be tearing off the flip chart sheets with the common themes and moving them to a visible location. Or it could be everyone doing High 5's, showing thumbs up, or shouting a group cheer, such as *Yeah! Woo Hoo! Wow!*

CONTRIBUTOR ROLE

At this step, there is an opportunity for a profound shift in your perspective. Any pre-meeting fears you may have had of losing your individuality in the collaboration process or being overpowered by other's ideas is now replaced by wonder at how ideas have blended together for a collective result. Similar to how a single drop of rain becomes the ocean, each individual experiences him or herself as both an individual contributor and a co-creator of the whole. You may not even be able to remember which ideas were yours and which came from others. We recommend that you:

1. Pause and reflect on the experience that has occurred as well as the information shared. Allow yourself to feel gratitude for what has been created.

2. Recognize that you did this, and the group did this; that the outcome is both your own and owned by the group. Let it in, let it blend. You have become a co-creator. You came into the conversation with your individual ingredients and ideas and you leave with a whole soup.

3. Celebrate what you and the group have co-created.

Hot Tip

Appreciate what has been co-created, no matter what it is or how it matches your expectations. Not every collaborative conversation will be a "10." Just as in cooking a soup, there may be too much or not enough spice, or some vegetables you don't care for. However, it can still be a very nourishing meal.

❦

Don't Settle -- Go For That Moment of Oneness

We had a six-month contract to teach collaborative skills to six tourist related organizations in a small town. They needed to agree on and implement actions that would bring more tourists to their city. When it came time to agree on an important marketing decision, discussing meaningful questions helped. However, for this group the key was continuing to get all the ideas out and re-visiting the common themes, several times, over several meetings. They finally agreed to move forward on one particular strategy, but there wasn't much enthusiasm for it. We didn't let them settle. Just when they thought they'd exhausted all possibilities, that "Aha!" moment occurred. A brilliant idea, which was an integration of what each had been saying, popped out. Instantly everyone gave it a thumbs up. Their excitement about finding a creative solution they all loved surprised them. Their confidence in the group's co-creative abilities grew, and they became willing to take on even more difficult projects.

We pushed them because we know that a creative breakthrough is often just on the other side of a group "hitting the wall."

Step 5: Plan the Action

Your collaboration soup has been planned, the ingredients brought together, the soup cooked and eaten. It is time to digest all that has happened and use the energy generated to turn the group's ideas into actions.

A key for this step is to bring a balance of both patience and momentum to the table. Just as when sharing a meal, some people will be more ready than others to leave the table and move on. The action-oriented people are ready to define what actions are to be taken, while the interaction-oriented people may want to linger for further conversation. An effective collaborative conversation requires patience on the part of everyone to allow for a balance of both.

FACILITATOR ROLE

Your role is to help the group shift their focus from contributing ideas to discussing possible actions.

Hot Tip

Be sure to allow enough time at the end of your meeting for the group to create their action plan, agree on next steps, and identify who will do what. Do not try to squeeze action planning into the last few moments.

1. Get agreement from the group to begin forming an action plan. Here are some questions you might ask:
   - Do we have enough common themes and ideas to begin creating an action plan?
   - Which of these ideas are we ready to take action on?
   - Reflecting on the purpose of today's conversation, are we ready to move forward?
2. Lead a discussion that helps the group create an action plan. If the group is large, you may want to break into small groups by topic or issue. For details on Formats for Organizing Input and Charting Action Plans see Part III: Tips and Tools. Make sure the following are included for each topic:
   - What will be done, by whom, and by when.
   - Identify sub-teams or committees, if needed.
   - If an action is assigned to a person not in the room, make sure someone present will communicate and follow up with him or her.
   - List resources needed, and the available or desired support (human, financial, etc.).

Hot Tip

Not every idea needs an action plan at this time. Focus on creating action steps for the topics where at least one person is willing to take responsibility.

3. Confirm what the next steps are, in writing. Be clear on who is accountable to do what and by when.
4. Determine when and how any follow-up meetings and/or communications will occur related to the action plan items.
5. Clarify what will happen with items that are not part of the group's action plan, yet still need to be addressed.
6. Clarify what will happen and who will follow-up on those items posted in the chart referred to as the "parking lot" in Step 3.

CONTRIBUTOR ROLE

Your job is to continue contributing as the conversation shifts from ideas to actions. Just as after a meal when energy leaves the brain and goes to the stomach, there is a tendency at this point in meetings to become sleepy or be distracted. Everyone needs to stay awake, engaged, and involved in order to turn the co-creative discussion into co-created action.

1. Take responsibility for moving some part of the action plan forward. You may choose a specific task or project that is part of the action plan and sign up for it, or support others in doing so.

2. Hold yourself and others accountable for what you say you will do. If you agree to do something, be clear what you are agreeing to, and do it.

No Action Plan = No Action

We attended a community meeting organized by a group of well-meaning volunteers. They hoped like-minded people would meet, generate ideas, and start neighborhood projects. The people leading the meeting explained the issues well. They asked people to gather in small groups by geographic area. However, the groups did not receive detailed directions about determining or recording next steps. A few people began to dominate, the conversations wandered, and people started to leave. There was no closing conversation about what projects were proposed.

We noticed how the hope and enthusiasm people expressed as they arrived had changed to confusion and frustration as they left. After the meeting, we asked the organizers why there was no closing discussion or summary of possible projects. They explained that they had planned to have the small groups come back together and discuss what actions they wanted to take, but had run out of time.

When people are ready to take action, it is essential to allow enough time at the end of a meeting to confirm what will happen next, and who is willing to take on what tasks.

Step 6: End with Clarity

Once the meal is over, it's time to clean up and put things in order. Nothing dampens the creative cooking urge more than walking into a kitchen to find dirty dishes, pots or pans left over from the previous meal.

Similarly, when your collaboration event is over and an action plan has been determined, cleaning up is the last step. This includes confirming the group's next steps, inviting closing comments, and making plans for creating and distributing the meeting notes, which we call the Summary Document. In addition to being a written record, a Summary Document, like a photograph, is a visual reminder that keeps the memory alive.

CONVENER ROLE

As the convener and/or the event planning team, you may want to make some closing remarks. Thank people for their time and participation. It is beneficial for the convener or event planning team members to recap why they wanted to have this conversation. Comment on what has taken place—perhaps what has moved you or what has been meaningful. The convener's heartfelt sharing is like a sweet mint at the end of a meal.

FACILITATOR ROLE

Your job is to bring the meeting to completion by doing the following:

1. Identify how the meeting summary will be compiled and distributed. For further details on Creating a Summary Document see Part III: Tips and Tools.
2. Clarify if there will be future meetings. If so, agree on when, who will host them, who the planning team will be, who will be invited, and how people will be notified.

3. Lead a brief closing discussion. Help people review and reflect on what has happened and what they have experienced. Examples of questions you can ask are:
   - What was accomplished here?
   - What did we learn?
   - What benefit did you (or we) gain from participating?
   - What are you taking from this event for use in other situations?
   - What might we do differently next time?
   - What made this gathering work?
   - How would you describe your experience here today?
4. Discuss how and what to communicate to people not present who may be interested.
5. Ask volunteers to help re-set the room, take down the charts, etc.

Hot Tip

Put discussion points, common themes, and action plans in writing and distribute a Summary Document widely after the event. Don't assume everyone will remember what was discussed in the same way.

CONTRIBUTOR ROLE

Your job is to continue to be a positive contributor. Don't physically leave or mentally check out before the end of the meeting. After the event is over and you receive the notes:

1. Check the Summary Document for accuracy. If there is anything that differs from your understanding or memory, let those who have prepared the notes know immediately.
2. Make sure you follow through on the actions you agreed to do as part of the action plan, support others in doing so, and continue communicating.
3. Assist others in accomplishing their tasks rather than judge or blame, or get alignment that it no longer needs to be done.

4. Communicate. Let people know when your task is complete. If you cannot do what you agreed to, or do it in the time agreed, let people know and discuss alternatives. You may need to find someone else to do what you promised to do; or get agreement that it does not need to be done. Forward any useful or relevant information.

∞

Re-Capping Saves Money and Reduces Conflicts

A city department hired me to help them increase the coordination among several of its divisions. They needed to work more collaboratively to accomplish some very expensive and far-reaching projects. The managers were concerned that people were duplicating other's work, not doing what was agreed, and giving different messages to their customers and vendors.

At my urging, they started allocating ten minutes at the end of each meeting to re-cap and clarify what was agreed and to identify who was accountable for next steps. They also made sure someone was accountable to send out meeting notes. Their managers were amazed at the increase in efficiency, teamwork and respect that occurred from that one small, ten minute change.

Simply summarizing at the end of a meeting what was agreed, and then quickly sending out meeting notes to everyone can avoid many conflicts.

So there you have it, the basic steps for an effective collaborative conversation. What follows in Parts III and IV are our favorite practices, tips and tools that we use in our collaborative consulting business. These will help you implement many of the directions given in Part II.

Part V contains two charts for troubleshooting difficult situations, because even with the best intentions, methods and skills, there are still situations that may require special attention. We have encountered many of these situations and offer our recommended solutions.

In our ongoing commitment to encourage and support effective collaboration and co-creative conversations we invite you to visit our website (www.collaborationsoup.com). There you will find stories and examples as well as our up-to-date recommendations, including books, trainings, websites, and other resources to help you. We encourage you to post your favorite tips and tools, your stories, and your questions. Become part of our Collaboration Soup community.

PART III: TIPS AND TOOLS

Part II contains the basic directions for each of the six steps in the *Collaboration Soup* recipe and the responsibilities for the various roles in each step. In Part III, we include tips and tools to help you implement each of the six steps in the recipe. This section includes:

A. Sample Agenda
B. Deciding How to Decide and Defining Alignment
C. Setting up the Room for Success
D. Note Taking & Using Flip Charts
E. Formats for Organizing Input and Charting Action Plans
F. Creating a Summary Document

Sample Agenda

It is helpful to put your agenda plan in writing, including allotted times, while staying flexible to make in the moment changes. Be sure and plan enough time for each section. Include details on what processes you plan to use and what supplies or support will be required for each step so you can be prepared. How much time you allot for each section will depend on:

- How many people are attending
- How well they know each other
- How similar or diverse the perspectives

Here is a sample form we use. This example is for a two hour meeting, 20 people or less.

START TIME	LENGTH	ACTIVITY	WHO	PROCESS/ MATERIALS/ NOTES
		BEFORE THE MEETING		
6:30		Arrive & set up room		
7:30		Be ready for arrivals	Greeters	
		WELCOME		
8:00	:05	Welcome • Background, including purpose • Explain your role • Introduce facilitator	Convener	

START TIME	LENGTH	ACTIVITY	WHO	PROCESS/ MATERIALS/ NOTES
8:05	:20	OPENING		
		Opening • Brain lifter or introductions • Logistics • Guidelines • Align on agenda • Agree on decision-making method	Facilitator	
8:25	:50	COOK THE CONVERSATIONS		
		Question #1 discussion		Example: Idea Board & Sticky Notes
		Question #2 discussion		Example: Small groups by topic
9:15	:10	INTEGRATE THE IDEAS		
		Summarize common themes		
		Acknowledge & celebrate		
9:25	:15	PLAN THE ACTION		
		Confirm next steps		
		Clarify who and by when		
9:40	:20	END WITH CLARITY		
		Confirm creation of the Summary Document		
		Closing discussion • Individual comments • Future meetings? • Communications plan		
10:00	:20	Clean up the room and put away materials		

Note: You can print a copy of this form from our website (www.collaborationsoup.com) to assist you in your planning.

Deciding How to Decide and Defining Alignment

Be sure you clarify and communicate who has final decision-making authority. If decisions are going to be made by the group during your event, it is important for the group to understand and align on how those decisions will be made. The facilitator may suggest a method or facilitate a discussion that considers various options. Agree on how ideas that do not receive agreement or alignment will be reported.

Here are some options and methods:

1. *Voting.* You can agree on what percent the group needs to agree for a decision to be made. Is 100% agreement needed or is a lower percent acceptable? Different percentages of agreement may make sense for different topics. This can be determined as you go.
2. *Alignment.* Rather than voting, you can seek to identify where there is alignment. Alignment means that people are willing to move in the general direction, even if they are not in complete agreement. To determine alignment, you can ask:
   - Is this acceptable?
   - Can you live with this and support it?
   - Is it close enough?
   - Can we go with this for now and revisit it if it becomes an issue?
3. *Thumb Voting.* To get a feel for how much alignment or agreement the group has, you can take a "thumb vote."

THUMB VOTING

A simple and quick way to assess alignment and to make any necessary alterations in what has been proposed is to have people vote with their thumbs. This is a way for people to air their concerns without voting against anything and for differing viewpoints to be heard and included. Here's how to do a thumb vote:

1. Clearly state the item or wording that is proposed. Ask people to hold up one thumb to indicate as follows:
   - Thumb straight up if they are willing to go with what has been proposed.
   - Thumb straight down if it is unacceptable.
   - Thumb sideways if they are lukewarm or need more information before agreeing.
2. For those with a thumb down or sideways, ask:
   - "What is your concern?"
   - "What information is missing?" or
   - "How could the wording on this be broadened or changed to include your ideas or get your agreement?"
3. Each time you receive a new suggestion, do the thumb vote again until alignment is reached or an acceptable solution is found.

Setting Up the Room for Success

It is important to create an environment for your meeting that has people feel at ease and comfortable. When people feel safe, they are more likely to access modes of thinking that support and encourage collaboration. In terms of brain science, you want to create an environment that helps people move into their higher, prefrontal cortex areas of the brain and away from defensive amygdala thinking (see Part I: Your Collaborative Brain). For example, make sure everyone can see, hear, and sit comfortably. Do your best to minimize external environmental factors or distractions. Here are some additional specifics:

1. **Arrive Early**
   - The set-up team and the facilitator should arrive in plenty of time to do what needs to be done and to take care of surprises.
   - Never assume that the directions or diagrams you have given to others for room set up have been translated properly.

2. **Greeters**
   - Welcome everyone warmly as they arrive. This sends a message that they are important and helps put them at ease.
   - If everyone doesn't know everyone, have nametags displayed in alphabetical order that show first names in large type. Or have blanks for people to fill out as they arrive.
   - Have a few people identified and available who can respond to questions and/or concerns, and who will communicate those to the convener or facilitator before the program begins.

3. **Information**. Have signs posted and clear information available as people arrive to help them get oriented.
   - Post a simple agenda on the wall with ending time.
   - Hang charts where they are highly visible and written in VERY LARGE print in dark colors.
   - Have background information available as handouts or posted on the wall in large enough print.

4. **Chairs and Visibility**. The more people can see each other's faces, the better. This will help build connection, trust and camaraderie.
   - Try to set the chairs so everyone can see everyone's eyes (or at least many people's eyes). Circles, arcs, pentagons, hexagons, or sergeant stripes are all options. Round tables work very well for small groups. If you must have rows, then curve them.
   - Minimize barriers between people, including tables.
   - Chairs with hard seats and without back support are uncomfortable for many people. If possible, have a few different kinds of seat options. If no alternatives are available, offer cushions, or be sure to not have people sit too long at one time without a break.
   - If there are observers who are not participating, have a few chairs set up in the back of the room for them.

5. **Sound**. Make sure everyone can hear what is being said.
   - Microphones are useful unless the cords, echoes or screeches become a distraction. Hand-held, cordless microphones are preferable, because they can be easily given to participants. Hand-held or lapel microphones are best for facilitators, because they can move around easily and still be heard by all.
   - Music influences the mood, so use it purposefully. Played softly in the background during the breaks, it can be useful for setting a tone and relaxing people. Upbeat music or music with appropriate lyrics can energize people.
   - The sound of water is also very relaxing – consider bringing in a small, portable fountain.

6. **Air.** Oxygen and temperature in the room are very important.
   - If possible, have a window open all or part of the time. If you are in an air conditioned enclosed environment, you can:
     - Encourage people to go outside during a break to get some fresh air.
     - Open a nearby door to the outside and leave the door to your meeting room open.
     - Bring in some plants with large green leaves.
     - Bring in a fountain for running water.
     - Bring in an air-filtering device.
   - Temperatures change frequently in most rooms, and in any group people have different preferences. Watch for signs of sleepiness or closed body posture and adjust the temperature as often as you need to. A room that is a bit on the cool side is better than one too warm.

7. **Odors.** Because some people are allergic to specific scents or odors and preferences vary so widely, avoid air sprays or scented candles.

8. **Privacy.** Minimize distractions and create the illusion of privacy, even if it isn't actually private, by:
   - Face the chairs away from any distractions.
   - Ask people not involved in the event to leave the area.
   - Put a sign up requesting privacy.

9. **Water and Food.** Sharing food together is a wonderful way to build bridges and create connections. It can be difficult for some people to concentrate when they are distracted by thirst, hunger, or cravings. Here are some tips:
   - Always have water available, even for short meetings.
   - While some people require caffeine or sugar to think clearly, do provide additional choices. Non-caffeinated tea is a wonderful addition to coffee.
   - For longer meetings, we suggest having a variety of snacks that includes protein (cheese or nuts), carbohydrates (bagels, pretzels or crackers), and sugar (fruit juice, whole fruit, or chocolate). Granola bars are easy, low cost, and can contain all of the above.

Note Taking and Using Flip Charts

When people's ideas are written for all to see, they feel respected. It confirms that their ideas have been heard and that they will be integrated into the meeting summary. Place the flip chart easels you are writing on in front of the group. Having a written record in front of the group can reduce repetition, and seeing the same visual gives them a common focus.

Be sure to have a good supply of poster paper, flipcharts, pens, markers, sticky notes and tape available during the event. These are useful for the recorders or facilitator to write what people say in easy-to-read, large print. Post the charts around the room.

Here are some tips for using flip charts:
- Use LARGE, BOLD, legible printing. Letters a minimum of 3 inches high are a good standard.
- Use wide marking pens that are non-toxic.
- Write the words people say, adding nothing of your own. You don't have to include every word they say, but substituting different words that mean the same to you can appear to be disrespectful. Substituting words should not be done without the speaker's permission and the recorder should check with the speaker to make sure what they meant was written accurately.
- You can use checkmarks to indicate when one person says something similar to another, with their permission.
- It is not necessary or advisable to put a person's name next to an idea unless they are agreeing to take an action related to it.
- Alternating two or more colors makes it easier for people to read the chart, and also stimulates creativity.

- Graphics can help people understand information because both the creative and rational parts of the brain are involved. Even something simple like bullets, circles or shading helps. Go ahead and attempt a drawing of anything – a star, a goal post, or even stick figures.

Formats for Organizing Input and Charting Action Plans

Visibly capturing the content of discussions, common themes, and action plans is important. A simple chart or an Excel spread sheet can work fine for any of these. Below are examples of formats we have used. If individual ideas have been grouped into categories, use the category name that the group has agreed upon, listing individual ideas beneath it as shown below.

SIMPLE ACTION PLAN FORMAT		
WHAT	WHO	WHEN
Review existing customer feedback forms	Charlie	September 30
Present summary of customer's top complaints	Charlie and Susan	Next Managers' meeting

THREE OTHER FORMAT POSSIBILITIES

Using the question "How Could We Provide More Art Education for Our Children?" as an example, the following are three different formats all using similar data.

VERTICAL LIST OF ACTIONS FOR INDIVIDUAL STRATEGIES			
STRATEGY 1 Advocate for Schools to Do It	STRATEGY 2 Recruit Volunteer Mentors	STRATEGY 3 Supply Stores Sponsor Classes	STRATEGY 4 Government Parks & Recreation Events
Contact Superintendent	Get artists invited into classrooms	Ask stores to participate— maybe donate a certain % of sales if people come in and mention the school	Retired artists teach classes for free, or a minimal amount.
Email our kids' teachers	Do art in after school programs	Publicize stores who provide a free class to kids if over $10 is spent in the store.	Put fliers at existing Parks & Rec classes to advertise classes at stores, and recruit mentors
Schedule pilots	Create a list of possible mentors	Create a roster of stores	
Train volunteers	Send an email inviting people to Mentor		
Conduct pilots	Contact service organizations		

HORIZONTAL LIST OF ACTIONS FOR INDIVIDUAL STRATEGIES WITH CALENDAR

DATE STRATEGY	JANUARY	FEBRUARY	MARCH
Advocate for Schools to Do It	Contact Superintendent	Email our kids' teachers	Schedule pilots
Recruit Volunteer Mentors	Create a list of possible mentors	Contact service clubs to announce this	Send email inviting people to participate
Supply Stores Sponsor Classes	Create a roster of stores	Ask stores to participate	
Government Parks & Recreation Events	Put fliers at existing Parks & Rec classes to advertise classes at stores, and recruit mentors	Retired artists teach classes for free, or a minimal amount	

SUB-TEAM ACTION PLANS WITH CALENDAR

MONTH	MARCH	APRIL	MAY	JUNE	JULY	AUGUST
TEAM NAME AND ACTIONS	*Advocate for schools to do it*	Contact Superintendent for permission	Email teachers w/ ideas	Follow-up with teachers & schedule for the Fall	Train volunteers	Publicize and recruit
TEAM MEMBERS	*Jerry T. Sandy S.*					
DESIRED RESULT	*More Art Education in classroom*	Superintendent agrees	Teacher says yes	Events are scheduled	Enough volunteers	Enrollments

Creating a Summary Document

The Summary Document contains all of the information and agreements made at the event or meeting. It should be sent out as soon as possible to all attendees, preferably within a week of the event. It can also be made accessible through posting on the Internet or other ways. If the technology and human power are available, it is wonderful to have someone input the data during the meeting, so that everyone can leave with a printout of the Summary Document.

At the end of the event, during Step 6: End with Clarity, identify the following:
- Who will be assembling and/or transcribing the notes to make a document?
- Who is responsible for sending out the document?
- Who will the document be sent to? We recommend sending it to everyone who attended the meeting. Fully disclose who, other than the attendees, will receive the notes and ask participants who else they think should receive it.

We recommend the document include:
- A brief history about how the meeting came about, including names of the convener and event planning team, why the conversation was initiated, any financial sponsors, and how it was determined who would be invited.
- The raw data as well as the common themes.
- Action plans and decisions, including timelines and accountabilities.
- Subjective observations or recommendations of the convener, facilitator or event planning team.
- List of attendees with a roster of their contact information, if permission has been given for their information to be shared.

PART IV: OUR FAVORITE METHODS, PROCESSES AND ACTIVITIES

In Part IV, we offer methods, processes, and activities to choose from in conducting your collaborative events. We have found the ones included here to be efficient, effective and easily adaptable to a variety of circumstances and sizes of groups. The directions are simple, and people generally enjoy their interactions as well as the results these methods produce.

There is no hard and fast rule about what to use when. Use the ones you are comfortable with. Take into consideration how much time you have, as well as how well people know each other and the intensity of the topic. Here is what follows:

A. Arrival, Brain Lifter and Opening Exercises

B. Helpful Facilitation Phrases

C. Creating Good Discussion Questions

D. Using Partners

E. Using Small Groups

F. Listening Circle

G. Idea Board Using Sticky Notes

H. Four Step Conversation

Arrival, Brain Lifter and Opening Exercises

Staggered Arrival Questions

Because people arrive at different times, it can be awkward for them to stand around without direction. Those who are early, or on time, can become irritated if the program does not begin on time. To put people at ease and get them involved as they arrive, use "staggered arrival" directions or questions posted visibly for them to see as they enter the room. You can request they answer the question(s) by writing on large flip charts that have been provided or by pairing up with others.

Here are some suggestions for staggered arrival directions and questions:

- Introduce yourself to two people you do not know and discuss what brought you here.
- What have we already accomplished, or what are we proud of, related to this topic?
- What are some outcomes you want to see from today's meeting?

Opening Brain Lifter

After you have welcomed people and thanked them for attending, find a way for everyone to speak and add their voice to the group. Structuring an opportunity to do this when people first come together helps create familiarity and opens pathways to the higher prefrontal cortex part of our brain referred to in Part I. When people share and learn about each other, they begin to notice their similarities. This builds a sense of safety and builds relationships. You can do this in several ways, considering the size of your group, how much time you have for this part, and how important it is to build relationships.

Here are some suggestions:
- Have each person say his or her first name to the whole group.
- Have each person turn to someone they don't know, or form a small group of three to four people, and introduce themselves.
- If you have time, in addition to their names, you can have them answer a specific question or two. For example: "Why is this topic important to you?" or "What is your hope for today's meeting?"
- It is sometimes helpful to ask unrelated "fun" questions, such as, "What is a favorite vacation spot?" or "Who is one of your heroes and why?"

Sometimes, giving people an opportunity to say what they are thinking as they arrive supports them to be fully present and focused. You can ask the question, "What does anyone need to say about anything, other than today's topic, so you are ready to proceed?"

Getting to Know You

Having people get up and move to greet each other and talk face to face is a great way to support people in feeling connected. Here are two easy and fun ways to do that:
- Shake hands. Announce that there will be a short period of time (1-3 minutes) for everyone to go around the room, shake hands, look each other in the eyes and say their name. Make it a contest to get to everyone as fast as possible and it will increase the energy in the room substantially.
- "Six degrees of separation" is a more interactive exercise where people meet and search for commonalities. Have them move around the room and at a signal from the facilitator rotate pairing up with someone, preferably someone they do not know or do not know well. Give each pair no more than two minutes to identify someone they know in common or something they have in common, outside of the topic of the day. Use a timer, whistle, or clap your hands to indicate when it is time to find new partners.

Helpful Facilitation Phrases

Asking questions in a sincere and respectful way can help people clarify or explore what they are trying to say. Often this leads to new insights. The following is a list of helpful phrases that can be used by the facilitator or by a contributor who is seeking greater clarity:

1. **Acknowledging**
   - "It sounds like .... is important to you."
   - "Am I correct in hearing that your experience with ... has been frustrating?"

2. **Encouraging**
   - "Can you say more about .... ?"
   - "We have heard from several of you. I am wondering if someone we haven't heard from has something to say about this."

3. **Clarifying**
   - "Can you explain more about .... ?"
   - "Can you give an example of .... ?"
   - "I would like to understand your idea, but I'm a little unclear about ...."

4. **Reflecting or Empathizing**
   - "When he said... it sounds like you felt ...."
   - "It sounds like you have a concern about ...." Or, "It sounds like you have a need to...."

5. Validating
   - "It sounds like you want to make sure that ...."
   - "I hear that it is very important to you that...."

6. Summarizing
   - "Let me see if I understand what you said. What I think you said was (restate their words)..... Is that correct?"
   - "You have made a number of points. Let me try to briefly summarize what I heard you say."

7. Reframing
   - In response to a negative comment, such as, "No one ever follows through on tasks," you could restate it in a more positive way, such as, "Would I be correct in saying that you want some assurance that people will complete the tasks assigned to them?"

8. Changing topics
   - "I am noticing the conversation shifting to a new topic. Is the group ready to move on, or is there more about the previous topic we need to discuss?"
   - "If we are ready to move on, can we take a moment to summarize what we have discussed so far?"

9. Guidelines not being followed
   - "In the beginning, we agreed to speak one at a time. Is that something we want to revisit at this time?"

Creating Good Discussion Questions

The kind of questions you ask to get people talking can have a huge impact on the quality of the conversation. Use thoughtfully crafted questions that invite fresh thinking, create energy, and stimulate new and unexpected combinations of ideas and insights. These kinds of questions encourage people to access their higher brain (PFC), so new knowledge and creative, strategic thinking can emerge.

Think about the purpose of your discussion: Is the purpose to get everyone's opinions out? Is it to discover the common ground? Is it to get "out of the box" ideas? We suggest that before the meeting, the facilitator, and perhaps members of the event planning team, generate several possible discussion questions, and then assess each question by asking the following:

- Does it generate hope, imagination, creativity and new possibilities?
- Will it catalyze new thinking?
- Is it easy to understand?
- Is it focused enough?
- Is it within the influence of this group?

Here are some tips:

- Determine what kind of answers are wanted, e.g. ideas, steps to take, opinions, out of the box possibilities, etc.
- Select questions that encourage people to go beyond their first or usual answers.
- Avoid "Why" questions, which tend to direct people into the past and can stimulate blame and defensiveness.

- Phrase questions using words like *challenges* or *possibilities* rather than problems or obstacles.
- Avoid questions that steer people to the answers you have already decided.
- Avoid yes or no questions.
- Use "What" and "How" questions (see examples below).

Examples of Questions for Specific Purposes:

1. **To Identify a Shared Vision or Goals**
   - How would an ideal future look?
   - What are the shared goals?

2. **To Identify Common Ground**
   - What are the common themes?
   - What seems to be emerging from the answers?
   - What are the mutual interests?
   - How can the various ideas be integrated?
   - How are the ideas related?

3. **Brainstorm Ideas**
   - What are some alternatives?
   - What are some ways to accomplish the shared goal of .... ?

4. **Action Planning**
   - What would a satisfactory solution need to include?
   - What are some ways this group could solve that?
   - What would help the group move forward on this?
   - How might an action plan be structured that would respect and include the various needs that have been expressed?
   - How could the group support each other in moving forward?
   - Who will do that?
   - When will that be done?

Using Partners

Putting people into pairs gives them a chance to interact and integrate the subject by reflecting with a partner. Here are some situations in which talking with a partner can be beneficial:

- When people are hesitant or shy to speak to the whole group
- When everyone has something to say and there isn't time enough for everyone to speak to the whole group
- When there is a lot of emotion
- When you want people to feel more connected to other people in the room
- When you are encouraging people to meet and get to know each other

You can pair people:

- With someone they don't know
- With a person sitting close to them
- With a person in the room they think they disagree with
- With someone they particularly would like to get to know
- Using relevant demographics, e.g. pair tenants with landlords; government people pair with business people, etc.

How it works:

1. Give directions for how you want them to pair up, using the above suggestions.
2. Verbally and on a written chart that the group can see, highlight the topic or question for them to discuss.

3. Give a clear time frame and a halfway warning signal to insure that both people have had a chance to talk.

4. Ask them to have a two-way conversation or use more structure in taking turns, one talking while the other listens and then reversing.

Using Small Groups

Putting people into small groups creates opportunities for many people to contribute their ideas. Here are some situations where using small groups can be beneficial:

- When there are people in the room with different levels of understanding about the topic.
- When there are natural groupings because of experience, type of job, etc.
- When you want to encourage interaction among people with diverse ideas or experience.
- When there are different aspects of the topic that can be talked about separately.
- When everyone has something to say and there isn't time enough for everyone to speak to the whole group.
- When you want people to feel more connected to the other people in the room.
- When you are encouraging people to meet and get to know each other.

How to Sort People into Groups

We like to keep the number of people in a small group between five and eight. The following are various ways to coordinate the formation of groups:

Random. This is beneficial for getting diverse perspectives. Go around the room in order and have people count off up to the number that will be in each small group. People with the same number then become a group.

Or, as people arrive, give them a number or a colored card and group them according to that hand out.

Topic. Sort by topics related to the subject. The topics can be determined before the meeting or can come out of the whole group's discussion.

Tasks. People gather as a work group or action team.

Spontaneous. People in the group offer an idea for a small group topic, posting the title on the wall. After everyone who wants to has offered their suggestions, people gather according to which title they want to talk about. Someone agrees to be the facilitator if one is not provided, and someone agrees to be the recorder if one is not provided.

Rotating. Sometimes people want to be part of more than one group discussion. You can give each group a certain number of minutes to discuss a few designated topics. Or, have people choose and move to a different topic table. The former group leaves a record of their discussion, and the new group adds to it, or creates new material.

Ways to Review Conclusions of Small Groups with the Larger Group:

Collating. Each small group identifies their common themes. Then the common themes from each small group are combined to identify the common themes of the whole group.

Art Gallery. Each group posts a large chart with their conclusions, recommendations or action steps for everyone to see. Then everyone walks around, like at an art gallery, to view what others have written. You might have those looking add their ideas and suggestions to each chart. They could also write their name next to an action they are willing to help make happen.

Listening Circles

This method is extremely versatile and allows for quality listening about a specific topic or question. It is very effective for hearing each person's views in a time-efficient way and for identifying areas of agreement. It works best with less than ten people. If you have a large group, you can break them into smaller groups and combine their answers later. There are three roles:

- **FACILITATOR** keeps the group on track.

- **RECORDER** takes legible notes as directed and hands them in to the facilitator.

- **TIMEKEEPER** announces when each person's time is up. (Let them finish their sentence.)

STEPS:

1. Draft a few questions the group could discuss.

2. Confirm the group's agreement on the question, or use their suggestions to formulate a new question.

3. Instruct the group to take a minute of quiet so each person can think about and organize their answer. Here's a phrase you can use: "Take a minute to organize your own thoughts, so you can listen when others speak."

4. Every person shares their answer within the agreed upon time frame—usually 30-60 seconds per person is plenty. Here's a tip: If a timekeeper announces the number of seconds it takes for each of the first three people who share, others will usually adjust to the time limit.

5. As each person shares, everyone else just listens. Encourage the listeners to:

   • See the topic from the other person's viewpoint.

   • Notice what others say that they agree with, or what makes sense to them.

6. No one speaks twice until everyone has spoken once.

7. Do not allow debates, attacks or grandstanding.

8. After everyone has shared their perspective, open it to the whole group for a general discussion.

9. Have the group then identify their common themes, similarities, or top three ideas.

10. Encourage them to write their results on a large flip chart.

11. If there is more than one group, have them bring their results back to the whole group.

Idea Board Using Sticky Notes*

This technique works well when people have a lot of opinions or ideas, and it's not time efficient to hear everyone speak. It is a good choice if you want to get quick solutions without a lot of stories or explanations. The Idea Board works well with large numbers of people when you limit the items each person posts. Be sure you have a large, clear wall space. Test the wall before the meeting to make sure your sticky notes (Post Its) actually stick to the surface.

Before Starting

- Make sure each person has at least fifteen sticky notes and a wide colored marker.
- If you are using random column symbols (letters, numbers or draw- ings) to help sort incoming ideas, post them high on a wall before the conversation starts. Leave an extra 2-3 inches in between col- umn headings.

Introduction

- Explain the steps the group will go through.
- Agree on the question to be discussed.
- Write the question on a large flip chart where everyone can see it.

---

* Adapted from Institute of Cultural Affairs, www.ICA.org, Discussion Method featured in *Winning Through Participation;* Kendall/Hunt Publisher.

Ways to Ensure Participation

- Invite, encourage, or push people to participate—you want as close to 100% involvement as possible.
- Respect everyone's input.
- If someone tries to dominate, refocus them on the group task and remind them we want all ideas posted.
- As facilitator, keep your ideas to yourself. Do not agree, disagree or make value judgments about contributors' ideas. If you are a team member facilitating this exercise, you can post your ideas at the end if no one else has put them up.

Step 1. Individuals Brainstorm

- Each person writes several answers to the posted question, using a wide, colored marker. Tell them to write just **one idea per sticky note**, using no more than five words.
- If you have posted symbols, explain the symbols are meaningless and just for the purpose of putting similar ideas together.

Step 2. Post Individual Ideas

- If there are a large number of contributors, encourage them to start by posting their top three ideas. Let them know there will be an opportunity for them to post their additional ideas later, if no one else has.
- If you are using random symbols as category headings, direct people to start placing their ideas on the board, grouping similar ideas under the same symbol.
- If you are not using random symbols, direct people to place their ideas anywhere on the wall.
- Once several ideas are on the wall, encourage anyone to start putting similar ideas together.
- Note: If you attach sticky notes to the bottom of another when posting, it is easier to move a whole section at once.

Step 3. Create Clusters and Groupings

- Once several ideas are on the wall, either the facilitator or volunteers from the group can start putting similar ideas next to each other.

- If an idea is not clear, ask the author to clarify what he or she has written.
- If there is disagreement about which items to cluster, continue moving the sticky notes around until an acceptable arrangement is found. If needed, ask the writer of the idea which column best fits their intent.
- End up with six to ten groupings. You may have some single ideas that do not fit with anything else, and that is okay.

Step 4. Name the Groupings

- Ask people to discuss what the individual answers in that grouping have in common.
- Agree on a short title (1-4 words) that captures the commonality. Let them try a few out until you can sense alignment, or an "Aha!" occurs where you see everyone nodding in agreement. Often a song title, witty phrase, or image works well. Encourage the use of descriptive verbs and action words. For example: "Initiate open communication" is more descriptive than just "communication."
- Have someone write the title on a different color sticky note or draw a border around the title and place it above the column over the previous random symbol, if you have used one.

Step 5. Reflect and Celebrate.

- Ask the group what they think and how they feel about what they created.

Step 6. Plan the Action.

- To indicate priorities, you can have the group use their colored markers, colored dots, or stickers to indicate which ideas they think are the priorities. You can direct them to prioritize chronologically according to what they think should be done next or by importance.
- Have people write their names legibly on ideas they agree to do or those they are offering to help make happen.
- If you group the ideas horizontally, you can easily place dates above them and move the sticky notes around to form a chronological action plan.

Note: See sample charts in Part III: Formats for Organizing Input and Charting Action Plans.

Four Step Conversation*

Research has shown that successful discussions move through four phases in a particular order. We call this the F.E.E.D. method, for Facts, Emotions, Evaluations and Decisions. Examples of questions to ask at each phase are listed below.

Facts – Make sure everyone has the same information.
- "Is there anything anyone wants to add to the information that was handed out?"
- "What information is important for us to know, in addition to what has been distributed?"
- "What clarifying questions does anyone need answered before we move on?"

Emotions – Create a structure and allow time for emotions to be expressed and received respectfully. This will help keep emotions from becoming disruptive or distracting later on.
- "How is this option feeling to everyone?"
- "What are your reactions to this topic?"
- "What are some of the emotions in the room?"
- "What are the fears and concerns about this topic?"

---

* Adapted from Institute of Cultural Affairs, www.ICA.org, O.R.I.D. method featured in *Winning Through Participation;* Kendall/Hunt Publisher.

Evaluations – Consider many choices before making a decision. This often leads to options not apparent before, and people feel their ideas are being properly considered.

- "What are some actions we could take to accomplish our goal?"
- "What ideas do you have for ....?"
- "What are some options for ......?"
- "What would you suggest for ....?"

Decisions – Be inclusive and clear about what is being decided and how the decision will be made and carried out.

- "Which of these are most likely to satisfy our defined goal?"
- "What shall we move forward on?"
- "Who is willing to take responsibility for ....?"

PART V: TROUBLESHOOTING

Troubleshooting Difficult Situations

What if . . .

There may be circumstances during collaborative conversations when things don't go smoothly. That is the nature and the wonder of collaboration. DON'T WORRY! Often just when the group seems most stuck, a breakthrough to a new solution or idea is at hand.

The following are some challenges that may occur and some options that have worked for us.

CIRCUMSTANCES, ISSUES OR PROBLEMS	OPTIONS & SUGGESTIONS
STEP 1. READY TO GO	
What if I don't have an event planning team?	• Yes, you can plan it yourself. • Make sure you get input from stakeholders.
What if I don't know what a stakeholder is, or who they are?	• Stakeholders are individuals or groups who have an interest in the outcome and/or who may be impacted by any actions the group might make.
What if stakeholders don't answer the survey questions?	• Explain the benefits of answering your questions. • Make sure they understand how their answers will be used to form the agenda. • Do research on the internet, or talk to people who know the stakeholders to learn about their needs and concerns.

CIRCUMSTANCES, ISSUES OR PROBLEMS	OPTIONS & SUGGESTIONS
STEP 2. ENGAGE YOUR GROUP	
What if people do not RSVP to the invitation?	• Attendance increases if you call or send reminders in advance. • Ask people you know personally who also know them to follow-up.
What if someone wants to attend who is not invited?	• Include them if possible. • Be honest about why they are not invited. • Ask them why they want to be there, and respond to their concerns. • If you must say no, find out what they want to contribute. Ask them to give you something in writing you will bring to the group.
What if I'm not sure when I need a professional facilitator?	• Consider hiring a professional facilitator when: ▪ The leader of the group wants to participate as a contributor. ▪ People will not speak freely if the boss is leading the meeting. ▪ The person scheduled to lead the meeting is perceived to have a bias, strong opinion, or a particular outcome in mind. ▪ Ideas are expected to be so diverse, or in conflict, that structured professional methods will be necessary.
STEP 3. COOK THE CONVERSATION	
What if contributors are confused, or disagree, about the purpose of the event?	• Edit or change the purpose to be meaningful to those present. • Confirm the meeting purpose, apologize for any misunderstanding, and invite them to participate. • Make it okay for someone to leave. Note: • The event planning team may not have done an adequate job of understanding contributors interests beforehand. • The invitation may not have clearly stated the purpose.

CIRCUMSTANCES, ISSUES OR PROBLEMS	OPTIONS & SUGGESTIONS
What if people are angry or disruptive?	• Speak calmly to them. • Acknowledge their right to have their opinions and feelings. • Refer to the behavior guidelines agreed to at the beginning of the meeting. • Ask a specific question to help focus them. For example: "What do you want to happen with what you are saying?" Note: See also Helpful Facilitation Phrases in Part IV. • Ask them if they want to be part of the collaborative process, or do they just want a platform to air their grievance. If it is the latter, give them a time frame to be heard, and then move on. • If they sincerely want to be part of the collaboration, find a way to incorporate their perspective.
What if people say controversial or off the wall comments?	• Ensure all ideas are acknowledged. • Go ahead and write their ideas along with everyone else's. • Ask the group what to do with their comment.
What if, as facilitator, I get off track, distracted, or don't know what to do next?	• It's okay to be authentic and real about this. The group will help you. • Say "I'm a little lost here – I'd like some help in deciding what we do next." • Give the group a question to discuss with a partner or in a small group to give you time to consider options. • Check in with the event planning team.
What if there is too much disagreement or conflict to proceed?	• Suggest the people involved work on that point outside the meeting. • Get agreement to set aside that point and find a theme/issue/area on which people are willing to move forward.

CIRCUMSTANCES, ISSUES OR PROBLEMS	OPTIONS & SUGGESTIONS
STEP 4. INTEGRATE THE IDEAS	
What if someone is critical of someone else's idea?	• The criticism may be due to misunderstanding what that person's point is. If so, ask someone else to say what he or she thinks that person is trying to say. • If it is an actual criticism, have each person involved say what is good about the other's idea.
What if the group can't reach agreement, or even alignment, on the common themes?	• Identify what small part can be agreed upon, even if it's just agreeing that they want to agree. • Keep searching for wording that will work for everyone, or the majority that is agreed upon. • Remind people they would not even be having the discussion unless they had something in common. Identify what that commonality is. • Break the issue into smaller parts. • Consider breaking the group into smaller groups by areas of agreement. • Decide it's okay to have some disagreement and agree to disagree.
STEP 5. PLAN THE ACTION	
What if people are hesitant to take on responsibilities?	• Continue communicating the importance of their input. • Inform them what will happen with their input. • Ask: "What is going on here?" Asking this question neutrally can often bring out very important issues that will then lead the group to be ready to take action.

CIRCUMSTANCES, ISSUES OR PROBLEMS	OPTIONS & SUGGESTIONS
What if action plans are too complex, or too time-consuming, to be realistically implemented by the group present?	• Be realistic about what can be done. • Break the actions down into smaller steps. • Prioritize. • Don't let people sign up to do too many things. • Identify the next action someone will take rather than outlining a long list.
What if actions are assigned to people who are not in the room?	• Make sure someone who is present takes responsibility to communicate with the person not there and confirm his or her agreement.
STEP 6. END WITH CLARITY	
What if someone is dissatisfied with the outcome?	• Ask and respect the nature of their dissatisfaction, and try to incorporate their perspective. • Ask the group to state what results were accomplished.
What if someone wants to change what he or she agreed to do?	• Re-confirm who said they would do what. • Identify what their issue is. • Support them in seeing how they could do it. • Redistribute the task.

Recovering From A "Fight Or Flight" Takeover

The amygdala part of the brain we referred to in Part I can trigger "fight, flight or freeze" behaviors. Below are three situations that can affect your ability to think collaboratively, and what can be done about it:

- Perception of aggressive language or movements
- Events that remind someone of a previous stressful situation
- Perceived differences

SITUATION	WHAT TO DO	HOW TO DO IT
Perceived or actual aggressive language or movements.	Don't proceed until the situation is acknowledged and neutralized.	1. Remind everyone of the behavior guidelines. 2. Help the person feeling threatened to explain what is upsetting them, and to also see the situation from the other person's perspective. 3. Give the perceived aggressor an opportunity to say more about what their concerns or ideas are. 4. If there is physical danger, or someone is disrupting the event beyond what is manageable, have options for him or her to leave.

SITUATION	WHAT TO DO	HOW TO DO IT
Events remind one of a previous stressful situation.	Help individuals manage their responses.	1. Acknowledge the upset. 2. Encourage people to balance their emotions; for example to take a deep breath, get up and walk around, get some water, etc. 3. Invite the person to briefly say something about what they were reminded of in the interests of putting it behind. 4. Take the person aside and talk with them individually. 5. Take a break.
Perceived differences.	Help identify common ground.	1. Ask people to listen for what they can agree with. 2. Encourage people to listen in a way that creates a connection, for example: • Make eye contact. • Repeat what you heard and ask, "What did I miss?" • Acknowledge feelings as well as words. 3. Respect their right to have an opinion different from yours and agree to disagree. 4. Clarify or comment on the similarities. 5. Have each person say what is good about the other's idea.

Afterword – About Stone Soup Meetings

We congratulate you for your interest in collaboration and for your desire and efforts to bring more co-creative conversations into your businesses, communities and relationships. We know that bringing people together who have differing points of view to find commonality and access their collective wisdom can seem like a tall order.

We believe you have the basics for effective collaboration within you. You can combine your experiences, knowledge and skills with the proven recipe and directions in *Collaboration Soup* to accomplish great things. Imagine using collaboration in your workplace or community to:

- Create and implement new ideas
- Have efficient and energized meetings
- Understand complex information
- Have an organized and systematic approach to solving problems
- Build relationships of trust in which people feel respected and heard
- Resolve conflict
- Identify shared goals
- Experience more fun and joy

Just as the book was going into production, a colleague began referring to a meeting that uses our recipe as a "Stone Soup Meeting." You can learn more about this on our website (www.collaborationsoup.com). In addition, you will find examples, useful resources, and stories from our clients, facilitation projects and readers. We invite you to post your stories and questions as well. Consider yourself a member of an ever-growing community of collaborationists.

The world needs collaboration. It is the way of the future.

Acknowledgements

Collaboration Soup is, truly, a collaboration soup! So many people from a wide variety of professions and perspectives contributed in many different ways.

We were amazed at how each of the dozens of people who read the evolving manuscript saw something different. This book would not be what it is without their thoughtful comments, most of which have been included.

There were many catalysts and encouragers along the way, including Bob Banner of HopeDance.org and Rick London of United Way San Luis Obispo County.

Never having written a book before, we appreciate the knowledge and patience of our friend, professional editor, and writing coach Nancy Marriott. She smoothed our rough edges and helped us explain our ideas more clearly. She had confidence in the importance of this work and encouraged us to persist through its many, many rewrites.

Our simple description for effective and co-creative events builds on the work of many dedicated individuals and organizations, too numerous to mention here. Our colleagues from The Collaborative Edge; Charles Feltman, Brad Isaacs, Don Maruska, and Vicki Milledge, were early allies in expanding our traditional definition and practice of collaboration.

Our husbands, Paul Menconi and Dr. Arnie Horwitz, were by our sides every step of the way. They forgave us for the week-ends and hundreds of hours we spent in front of the computer, and for our endless promises that "we're almost done."

It is hard to put into words the awe and appreciation for our writing partnership. Our friendship since 1986 has been a source of support, wonder, and co-creation in many circumstances. The experience of co-authoring this book has brought a new joy to our friendship and unimaginable depth to our consulting and facilitation business.

We thank all of you who are reading and using this book for being the magnet that helped tap our collective wisdom.

About Us . . .

Delia Horwitz and Paula Vigneault

We have been friends for over 20 years, as well as co-facilitators for many collaborative events. Our broad and diverse backgrounds mix well, whether we are shopping for clothes or designing a public event. Given our shared interests of fun, creativity and service, we were thrilled when we began to co-create this book.

The idea of writing a book came about quite unexpectedly, and the form and content evolved over a two-year period. It all began when a magazine publisher asked us to write a short article describing the keys to effective collaboration. Soon after, we were participants in meetings led by well-meaning people who wanted their group's interactions to be collaborative. After each experience, we discussed what we would have done differently that would have improved the results and enjoyment for everyone present. Then, the Executive Director of a local non-profit asked us to write a guide for self-facilitated collaborative groups. That sounded like a big task, and instead we offered to research existing publications on the topic. We could not find anything that had a concise overview of the keys we had written about, was easy to read, and simple to use.

We began to jot down on napkins and envelopes other ideas, expanding on the key points. We were waking up in the middle of the night with inspirations, and could not wait to find time to gather at the laptop and see what would emerge. Interestingly, the only way our writing flowed was when we were both sitting at the computer together. Individually writing sections and then trying to combine the two together was like each of us cooking a pot of soup and putting the two together – sometimes it worked, but more often the flavor of the words did not mix. We discovered our shared voice of "DePau," and DePau Productions was born.

We are enjoying continuing to co-create as authors, entrepreneurs, management consultants and professional meeting facilitators. Our husbands refer to us as *"The Soup Sisters."*

About Delia . . . Delia Horwitz has had extensive experience consulting and facilitating with hundreds of groups in a wide variety of circumstances, beginning in the late 1970's. Her projects include strategic planning with non-profit Boards of Directors, teambuilding with small and large corporations, goal setting with City Councils, corporate culture work with Fortune 500 senior leadership teams, and visioning with community stakeholders. She also co-founded and served for three years as Executive Director of Leadership Santa Barbara County. In addition to partnering with Paula on *Collaboration Soup*, Delia owns and is the principal of Business Relationship Consultants.

She is also the author of *The Achieving Agreement Workbook: Managing Your Internal and External Conflicts* and *Letters From My Future Self: Musings of a Mid-Life Seeker.*

About Paula . . . Paula Vigneault has had several careers working with and managing teams in the medical, construction and retail fields. As an entrepreneur, she founded and managed for 15 years a successful book and gift store in Santa Barbara, California. Paula has continually pursued her passion for collaboration and has volunteered her time with many non-profit groups as a Director, event organizer and meeting facilitator. Some of those projects include Women Waging Peace at the Harvard School of Government, Project Esperanza in Guatemala, and the International Dances of Peace Strategic Planning Conference in Holland with contributors from 20 counties. She now works as a SCORE volunteer, is a Hub member of SLO Transition Towns, and is co-owner of Energy Efficiency Solutions in San Luis Obispo.

You can reach us at www.collaborationsoup.com (805) 215-3717.

**